NO PLANET B

Camilla de la Bedoyere

Badger Publishing Limited
Oldmedow Road,
Hardwick Industrial Estate,
King's Lynn PE30 4JJ
Telephone: 01553 816083

www.badgerlearning.co.uk

2 4 6 8 10 9 7 5 3 1

No Planet B ISBN 978-1-78837-575-7

Text © Camilla de la Bedoyere

Complete work © Badger Publishing Limited 2022

All rights reserved. No part of this publication may be reproduced, stored in any form or by any means mechanical, electronic, recording or otherwise without the prior permission of the publisher.

The right of Camilla de la Bedoyere to be identified as author of this work has been asserted by them in accordance with the Copyright, Designs and Patents Act 1988.

Commissioning Editor: Sarah Rudd
Copyeditor: Carrie Lewis
Designer: Adam Wilmott

Cover Image: Shutterstock/Romolo Tavani
Page 5: Shutterstock/anut21ng Stock
Page 6: Juliet Breese
Page 7: Juliet Breese
Page 8: Shutterstock/TR STOK
Page 9: Shutterstock/Katiekk, Shutterstock/Katrien1
Page 10: Shutterstock/Vitalii_Mamchuk
Page 11: Alamy/Pulsar Imagens, Shutterstock/Katrien1
Page 12: Tao Wimbush
Page 14: Shutterstock/PradeepGaurs
Page 15: Shutterstock/Bennyartist, Juliet Breese
Page 16: Shutterstock/Creative Travel Projects
Page 17: Shutterstock/pingebat
Page 18: Shutterstock/Dado Photos
Page 19: Shutterstock/MarleenS
Page 21: Shutterstock/Petair
Page 23: Shutterstock/surassawadee
Page 24: Shutterstock/NinaMalyna
Page 25: Shutterstock/Rich Carey
Page 26: Shutterstock/Morinka
Page 27: Shutterstock/Clara Bastian
Page 28: Juliet Breese
Page 29: Juliet Breese

Every effort has been made to contact copyright holders of material reproduced in this book. Any omissions will be rectified in subsequent printings if notice is given to the publisher.

NO PLANET B

Contents

1. Time to Change	4
2. Who Lives Wild?	9
3. Energy Matters	13
4. Building Better	17
5. Travel	20
6. Food and Farming	24
7. My Wild Life	28
Glossary	30
Questions	31
Index	32

1. Time to Change

Words **highlighted in this colour** are in the glossary on page 30

Do you think you can change your life in a way that helps the planet?

One way to help would be to live sustainably. A sustainable life brings us closer to nature and is kinder to our planet. This type of living can be called green or eco-friendly.

Time to act

There are about 7.9 billion people alive today – more than ever before. In just 30 years there will be around 10 billion people. They will all need space to live, food to eat, clean air to breathe and natural resources for everyday life.

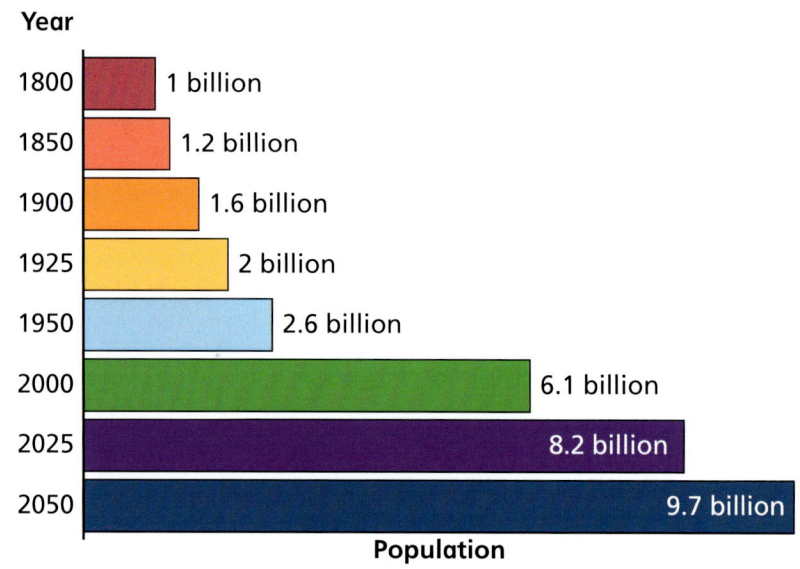

Year	Population
1800	1 billion
1850	1.2 billion
1900	1.6 billion
1925	2 billion
1950	2.6 billion
2000	6.1 billion
2025	8.2 billion
2050	9.7 billion

What is sustainable living?

Living sustainably means ensuring that we do not damage the planet for the people who live after us. We need to take care of our **environment** because there is no planet B for the people of the future.

What a waste!

Two billion tonnes of waste are thrown away every year – from food packets and nappies to last year's technology. In 30 years, it will double to four billion tonnes of waste.

Natural resources

Humans use the Earth and its materials to for many different purposes. These materials are called natural resources and some of them can never be replaced.

We use natural resources from underground, including rocks, minerals and fossil fuels.

We also remove natural resources from under the sea. Metals are mined from the ocean floor for items such as batteries. Oil can also be extracted to make petrol or plastic.

Wild animals and farm animals are natural resources that we use for food. We destroy habitats to use the land for farming, which can ruin the soil. We cut down trees to use the wood for building and manufacturing.

The use of natural resources is damaging our planet and causing pollution. The air that we breathe and our water sources need protection from this.

WOW! facts

In the last 30 years we have doubled our use of natural resources.

Change for the better

The good news is that we can live better lives. We can change the way we eat, travel and heat and power our homes. We need to think carefully about the things that we buy. We can improve how we care for the planet and should limit our use of its natural resources.

WOW! facts

90% of people worldwide breathe polluted air.

2. Who Lives Wild?

Living sustainably is not a new idea. In the past, all people lived this way and today there are still many people around the world who live sustainably in nature.

My name is Namelok, I am 14 years old and I live in a Kenyan village with my family. We are proud to be Maasai people.

Maasai people use cattle for almost everything. My job is to milk the cows and my brother takes the herd to find water and grass. When the cows have eaten all of the grass we move the herd to a new place, so the grass is not damaged and can grow back.

We eat beef and drink milk, we make spoons from cattle horns and bones and we use the **cowhide** to make clothes and shoes. We also use it to make walls and roofs for our home. We even use cow dung to make **plaster** for the walls. Nothing goes to waste.

Arctic living

Inuit people live in the Arctic where temperatures can drop to a freezing -35 degrees Celsius,, which means very few species can survive there.

In the past, Inuit people lived a sustainable lifestyle finding food by fishing and hunting. They used animal skins to make clothing, tools and boats, called **kayaks**, and they built igloos to shelter from snow and icy winds.

Today, many Inuit people have decided to live in towns, but staying close to nature and living a wild life is still important to them, so they can teach their children these traditional skills.

WOW! facts

Inuit people can build an igloo in less than an hour.

An Amazon life

My name is Mukashe and my people are the Yanomami of the Amazon rainforest.

We have everything we need in the forest. We hunt animals to eat, we forage fruits, seeds and nuts, and we grow crops of banana and corn. When supplies of food run low, we move to a new place so the food never runs out and the forest can recover.

We use trees to build our homes and plants as medicine. We also use plants to make hammocks, tools and baskets.

We only take from the forest what we need to survive. If we take too much, we risk damaging the environment around us that we rely on for survival.

Ecovillages

An ecovillage is a place where everyone tries to follow a sustainable life. There are more than 10,000 ecovillages in the world.

People who live inside ecovillages try to:
- build houses from sustainable materials
- use clean, green energy instead of fossil fuels
- grow food in a way that does not damage the environment
- recycle their waste
- take part in local projects to protect nature
- teach others how to live a sustainable life

Eco-houses in the Lammas ecovillage, Wales.

3. Energy Matters

Gas, oil and coal are fossil fuels which we use for energy and to generate electricity. They power our businesses and industries, our vehicles and our homes.

The use of fossil fuels harms our planet. When they burn, they release greenhouse gases into the air, such as carbon dioxide. These gases cause the planet to warm, which changes the climate. Greenhouse gases also pollute the air and damage our health.

There are other, greener ways to produce energy, such as solar power and wind power. They are called renewable energies as they will never run out.

Solar power
We can use the energy that comes from the sun and convert it into power using solar panels. Solar panels work best in places that have plenty of sunshine all year round.

WOW! facts
Solar power still only makes up about 3.2 per cent of the world's power.

Solar ovens

In parts of India, women have to cook on wood fires. They spend hours every day looking for firewood and cutting down trees. This harms the environment, and the wood smoke damages people's eyes and lungs.

Now, some people are using solar ovens instead of wood fires. A huge, reflective panel concentrates sunlight onto a metal box, which can be heated to temperatures of 150 degrees Celsius. This box is then used for cooking food, which is much more sustainable.

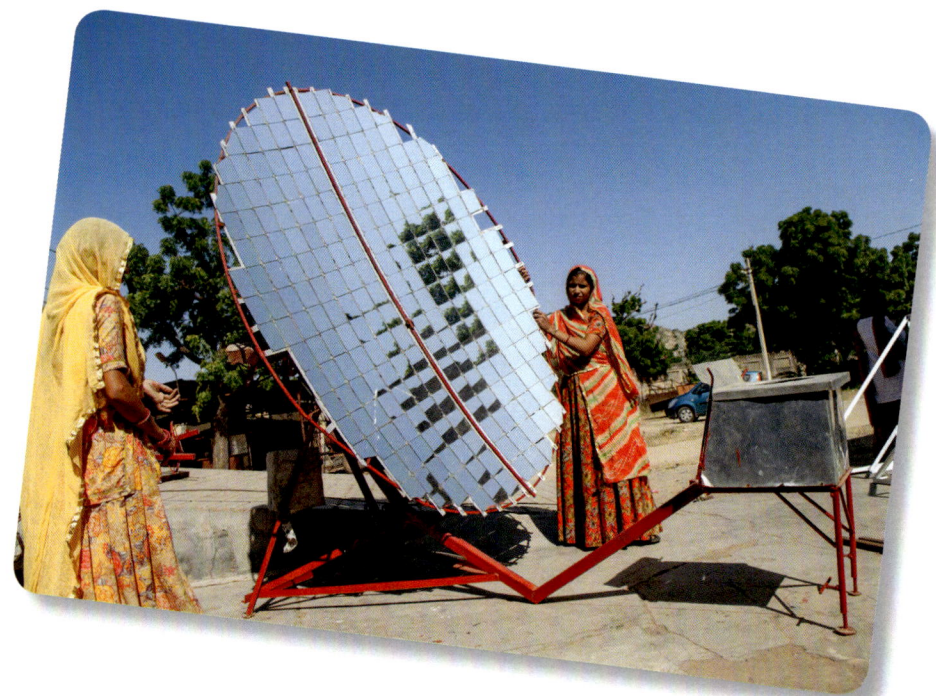

Wind power

For thousands of years, people have been using wind energy. Wind can power a pump to bring water out of the ground or turn the sails on a windmill to turn grain into flour. Today, wind power is used to make electricity.

Water power

Hydropower is energy that comes from moving water. When water flows downhill it can be used to make electricity.

WOW! facts
One wind turbine can make electricity for 500 homes.

A geothermal pool in Iceland.

Hot Earth

Geothermal energy comes from heat inside the Earth. Iceland and New Zealand have been using geothermal energy for many years, and it is becoming popular in other countries too.

Heat pumps can be used to take the heat from underground. They are a sustainable choice as they use very little fossil fuels to power the pump.

WOW! facts

Currently, only about 18% of the world's energy is renewable.

4. Building Better

A green home, or eco-building, is built with the idea that over its lifetime it will have a smaller **carbon footprint**. When people live in a green home they save water and energy – and money!

Big problems

Buildings use up almost 40 per cent of the world's energy. Some of that comes from putting up the buildings in the first place. However, most of the energy is spent on heating, cooling and lighting them.
- Trees are cut down for wood.
- Natural resources are dug out of the ground and used to make bricks and other building materials.
- Concrete and cement are materials that produce lots of greenhouse gases.

By 2050, about two-thirds of the world's population will be living in cities. Cities cover just 3 per cent of the planet's surface but they use up 78 per cent of the energy.

Taking action

In the future, builders will need to use materials that have been recycled or can be replaced. They will have to make sure that buildings use renewable energy and that they are **insulated**.

The Museum of Tomorrow

Brazil's Museum of Tomorrow is a building for the future. It helps visitors to imagine a sustainable world and explore ways they can help save the planet.

The museum has solar panels that can move to face the sun and uses water from a nearby bay to cool the air. There are pools, gardens, a park and bike lanes around the museum, as well as 15,000 trees.

Inside the building, visitors learn about:
- the way humans are affecting the planet
- **climate change**
- green energy
- how science can help us to help nature

Living walls

Some buildings really are green! Architects design them with 'living walls' that are covered in plants. The plants help absorb carbon dioxide, keep the building warm and they look incredible too.

WOW! facts

Research has shown that living walls can decrease stress in the workplace.

5. Travel

We use many sorts of vehicle to travel, such as cars, trains, boats and planes. Most of these vehicles use fossil fuels, which are not renewable. When they burn their fuel, the vehicles pollute the air and add to the problem of climate change.

Danger!
Diesel and petrol, which are used to power cars, vans, lorries and trains, are fossil fuels made from oil. When diesel and petrol burn they release greenhouse gases into the air. They also cause lung diseases, including asthma and cancer. About 90 million barrels of diesel and petrol burned in the world every single day.

Electric cars

Electric cars use batteries instead of burning fossil fuels. An electric car is plugged into a charging point. Electricity transfers to the car's batteries and is stored there. When you drive, this power is used by the motor.

Some electric cars also have a petrol engine so they can swap between using petrol or electricity. These are called hybrid cars.

Electric vehicles are a greener way to travel. However, the electricity they use might be generated by burning fossil fuels. The best electric vehicles use electricity that comes from clean, renewable energy, such as solar power.

WOW! facts

At the end of 2020 just 1 in 250 vehicles was electric. By 2040, 1 in 3 cars will be electric.

Active travel

Walking, running and cycling are greener, cleaner ways to travel. They are called 'active travel' as you have to be physically active to get from one place to another. Many towns are being designed so they are safe for active travellers.

Advantages	Disadvantages
✓ Great for the environment as it does not create pollution	✗ Not suitable for people with disabilities, or the elderly
✓ Cuts down the number of traffic jams in cities and towns	✗ Not all roads are safe for cyclists and pedestrians
✓ Helps people to keep fit and healthy	✗ At night, or in winter, conditions might not be safe
✓ Helps people to save money	✗ Some distances are just too far away to walk, run or cycle

How to Travel Green

- Leave the car at home and travel by foot or bike if possible.

- Share car journeys – one car on the road is much better than two.

- Use public transport, such as buses and trains.

- Think before you order a delivery to your door. How will the delivery driver travel?

- Think about holidays. Can you plan a greener way to travel when you go away?

6. Food and Farming

By 2050, our planet will be home to 2 billion more people. We must find ways to feed everyone without harming the planet. Sustainable farming is a way of growing food that doesn't damage the environment.

Soil matters

We need soil because it holds water and nutrients that plants need to grow and is a home for wildlife. Soil also plays an important part in climate change as it keeps our water clean, helps prevent flooding, and stores carbon.

When soil is over-farmed it becomes damaged. Sustainable farming keeps soils healthy, which means crops can grow successfully and the damage to the climate is minimal.

WOW! facts

More than one billion people work in farming around the world.

Chemical fertilisers or compost?

Farmers add chemical **fertilisers** to the soil to help plants grow. It takes a lot of energy to make fertilisers, and they damage wildlife. They also release greenhouse gases into the air. Sustainable farms use natural fertilisers, such as compost, to be kinder to the environment.

WOW! facts
Every year, about one-third of food that is grown or made for humans is wasted.

Forests or farms?

Forests are being cut down to clear the land for farming. This is called deforestation and it is bad for the climate. It destroys wildlife habitats, damages the soil and causes flooding.

Good food

Many people want to change their diet so it is more sustainable, but how easy is it to eat a healthy diet that is also kind to the planet?

In a sustainable diet:
- red meat is only eaten occasionally, or not at all
- meals are based on plants, especially beans, **lentils** and nuts to replace the protein in meat
- organic food is eaten when possible
- food from local farms is eaten, rather than from hundreds of miles away or even abroad

Why go plant-based?

Animals that live on farms, such as cows, pigs and sheep, are called livestock. About 15% of all our greenhouse gases comes from animal farming. Cutting down the amount of meat and dairy foods we eat is an easy way to reduce this.

When farm animals eat and then digest their food they make greenhouse gases, such as carbon dioxide and methane. Growing plants takes carbon dioxide out of the air and uses much less energy than farming animals.

WOW! facts
Farming one kilogram of meat uses the same energy as driving a petrol car for 155 miles.

7. My Wild Life

Simple steps

Here are some simple ideas to become eco-friendly and help save our planet. If we all make small changes to our lives, they will add up to make a big difference.

Save energy
Turning off light bulbs, chargers and gadgets when they are not being used can save electricity and money. If we all switched to using very low energy light bulbs we could stop 1400 million tonnes of carbon dioxide going into the air.

Save resources
Repairing and re-using things, such as clothes and furniture, is a great way to be sustainable. It means we do not have to make or buy new things, which would use more natural resources.

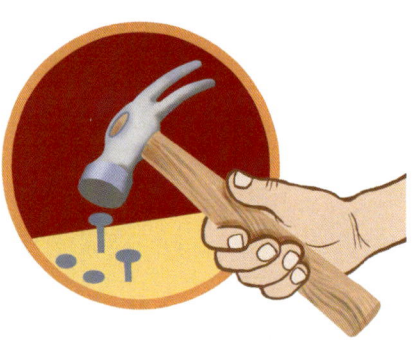

Cut waste
Recycling paper means fewer trees are cut down. Glass, fabric and many plastics can also be recycled, which saves natural resources.

Save water
Cleaning and transporting water uses energy so it makes sense not to waste it. A five-minute shower uses about 45 litres of water, but a bath uses twice as much as this.

Help wildlife
Growing flowers for bugs is an easy way to help the wildlife. You can also join local groups that clean or protect wildlife habitats.

Eat green
By eating less meat, even for one day a week, you can have a huge impact on the environment. You could even grow your own vegetables to eat and turn any food waste into compost.

GLOSSARY

asthma — a disease of the lungs that makes it hard to breathe

climate change — a change in global weather patterns due to an increase of greenhouse gases

cowhide — the dried skin of a cow

environment — the type of place that surrounds us, such as the air, the water and the soil

fertilisers — a substance that is added the soil to make things grow better

fossil fuel — a fuel containing carbon, made from the remains of prehistoric plants and animals

insulated — to cover or surround something with a material that heat, electricity, or sound escaping.

kayak — a lightweight boat that is pointed at both ends

lentils — seeds from plants that can be used as food

plaster — a paste made from lime, sand and water that hardens when it is put onto a wall

pollution — types of waste that are harmful to humans and the environment

Questions

Why do Inuit people build igloos? *(page 10)*

How many eco-villages are there in the world? *(page 12)*

Which two countries have been using geothermal energy for years? *(page 16)*

In which year will 1 in 3 cars be electric? *(page 21)*

Name three negative impacts that deforestation has on the environment. *(page 25)*

What percentage of greenhouse gases come from farm animals? *(page 27)*

INDEX

Amazon 11
building 7, 17, 18, 19
eco village 12
eco-friendly 4, 28
electric cars 21
energy 12, 13, 15-18, 21, 25, 27-29
environment 5, 12, 14, 19, 22, 24, 25, 26, 29
farming 7, 24, 25, 27
food 4, 5, 7, 10-12, 24-27, 29
fossil fuels 6, 12, 13, 20, 21
geothermal energy 16
Inuit 10
Maasai 9
metals 6
natural resources 4-8, 17, 28
pollution 7, 22
soil 7, 24, 25
solar power 13, 21
sustainable 4, 5, 9, 12, 18, 24-26, 28
travel 8, 20-23, 26
waste 5, 9, 12, 25, 28, 29
water power 15
wind power 15